COOKIN'

WITH

BEER

By Rick Black

Dedication

I dedicate this book to my Goddaughter **Alyssa Lyn Black**.
She knows her Uncle Rick is only kidding. Hey Mike, you and April did a good job!

Rick & Becky

© 2002 Rick Black

Table of Contents

You might notice that this book is just a tad skinny for a three hundred page book.

What happened is that my publisher told me either to do a three hundred pager, or get lost.

Well, I didn't have three hundred of stuff to say, so I started 'er out on page 157. I think I can get away with it. I'm not sayin' my publisher is sort of slow or anything............but he did go to 5th grade long enough to get tenure.

Preface

This is not your run of the mill girly boy cookbook.
A beer drinking, hell raising, downright cussing and fighting man wrote this book.
The reader will discover the fine art of cooking foods that include the nectar of the gods, BEER.

Along with tasty recipes, the reader will enjoy beer trivia and some of the funniest beer drinking jokes on paper.
The fact of the matter is that cooking with beer has been included in dishes that go back as far as the 25,000 B.C.

Yep, it seems beer has been around for a while and I would guess it would be here for sometime longer.

In this book I will share with you recipes on cooking beer with soup & stews, seafood, chicken, beef, pork, and my favorite *Mountain Man Cooking With Beer*!

This, like all my books, was written to be shared with family and friends.

The Truth About Beer And Deer

Billy and Rick went to the bar one afternoon. Billy was explaining his theory about beer and deer to his buddy Rick. And here's how it went:

" Well, you see Rick; it's like this...a herd of deer can only move as fast as the slowest deer. And when the herd is

hunted, it is the slowest and weakest ones at the back that are killed first.

This natural selection is good for the herd as a whole,

because the general speed and health of the whole group keeps improving by the regular killing of the weakest members.

In much the same way, the human brain can only operate as fast as the slowest brain cells. Excessive intake of beer, as we all know, kills brain cells, but naturally it attacks the slowest and weakest brain cells first.

In this way, regular consumption of beer eliminates the weaker brain cells, making the brain faster and more efficient. And that's why you always feel smarter after kicking back a few beers."

Introduction

If I only had a dollar for every time I heard the sound of my wife's voice screaming *"Why do you always want to put beer in our food!"*
Yep it was the same thing every day, every month, and every year.
So how did I get my lovely bride of 18 years to overcome her concerns about me cooking with beer?
The answer was with facts.

Some examples; did you know that the finest chefs and cooks serve famous dishes that include beer in some of the most prestigious restaurants in the world?

Cooking with beer has been around before the birth of Christ. Why? Because basically beer is known as liquid bread. And what better food element compares to bread?

To understand why beer makes such a great ingredient in cooking, one must know just what exactly is in beer.

Beer is made from the from the following four main ingredients:

1. Barley malt, which gives beer its fullness;
2. Hops, which gives beer its bitterness;

3. Yeast, which converts the barley malt into alcohol and carbon dioxide;
4. Water, which assists the fermentation process, distillation, and cuts down the final product into consumable proofs.

So now that we know just what goes into beer, lets find out why the ingredients listed, make beer such a good flavor to cook with.

1. ***Barley*** – Barley is to beer what grapes are to wine. Actually, any cereal grain such as corn, wheat, rice, oats, and rye work great in beer. The cereal grain gives the beer its color, sweetness, body, protein, carbohydrates, vitamins, and minerals. But more importantly, it gives the beer the starch, which is then converted into sugar, which is in turn transformed into alcohol and carbon dioxide by the fermentation process. Barley is by far the best cereal grain for beer flavor.

2. **Hops** – Hops is a plant, which is a member of the nettle family. It resembles a small green/yellow pinecone with soft leaves about an inch long. Hops are grown in many different climates and locations and each variety produces a beer with a different taste. Hops are added to the developing beer in two stages, the first for flavoring and the second for aroma.

3. **Yeast** – This is the stuff that makes the beer jump up and kick ya! The yeast attacks the malt sugar in the barley and converts in into alcohol and carbon dioxide. This is called fermentation. After fermentation, the yeast is removed.

4. ***Water*** – Another key ingredient in the flavor of beer. Be it soft, hard or spring, water does make a difference in the flavor of the beer. And it's the flavor of beer that makes the recipes your about to read in this book mouth - watering and fun to cook.

So get ready to have some fun. Because when it gets down to it, real men drink and cook with beer.

Cheers!

Rick

Soups and Stews

I have put together some of my favorite soup and stew beer recipes.

Although you may find several types of soups with similar names such as "chili", please read each one, because each will have it's own flavor and each is truly delicious.

Remember soup should be as much fun to make as it is to eat, so make sure and try them all with friends and family!

Tinker's Warm Beer Soup –

- 1 cup beer
- 1 cup milk
- 1 egg yolk
- 1 tablespoon sugar
- 2 whole cloves
- ¼ teaspoon cinnamon
- ½ teaspoon lemon rind
- 1 tablespoon flour
- 1 teaspoon seasoned salt

In a large pot bring beer to a boil. Add cloves, sugar, cinnamon, and lemon rind.
In another pan bring the milk to a boil add flour, seasoned salt and add this to the beer. Add egg yolk and stir on very low heat for about 5 minutes.

Rick's Tavern Soup –

- ½ cup chopped celery
- ½ cup chopped carrot

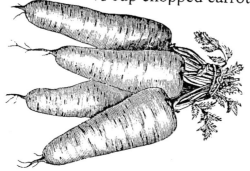

- ½ cup chopped green pepper
- 1 cup chopped yellow onion
- 3 cans chicken broth
- 3 tablespoons butter
- 1 teaspoon salt
- 1 teaspoon black pepper
- 1/3 cup flour
- 3 cups grated sharp cheddar cheese
- 1 can beer (room temp)

Combine celery, carrots, green peppers and onions in a slow cooker.
Add broth, butter, salt and pepper. Cover and cook on low for about 6 hours. Strain mixture; puree the vegetables in a blender and return to the crock-pot on high setting.
Dissolve flour in a small amount of water, add to broth, and add cheese slowly, stirring until well blended. Pour in beer, cover and cook on high for about 20 minutes.

Billy's Beer Potato Soup –

- 2 tablespoons butter
- 1 tablespoon garlic
- 1 cup chopped green onions
- 1 stalk diced celery
- 6 cups boiled diced red potatoes
- 1 qt beer (32 ounces)
- 1 tablespoon chicken boullion
- 2 large cans chicken broth (64 oz)
- 4 cups cream

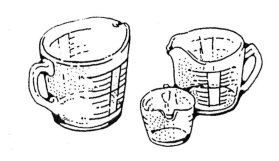

Sauté garlic in butter for about one minute, add vegetables and sauté for another 5 minutes or until tender.

Add potatoes and beer and bring to a boil. Mash potatoes against sides of pot.
Add sugar, broth, boullion and salt and pepper to taste.
Add cream, stir and serve.

Dick Black's Smoked Sausage, Beer and Cheese Soup –

- 1 pound sausage
- 1 can dark beer
- 3 chopped potato
- ½ pound shredded cheddar cheese
- ¼ cup white wine

- 3 cups water
- 1 tablespoon salt
- 3 diced green onions
- 1 cup heavy cream

In a large pot, boil potatoes until tender. Add onions, wine, salt and sausage.

Simmer until potatoes are completely tender. Add remaining ingredients and simmer for about 2 hours or until soup thickens.

Packer Fans Onion Soup with Beer –

- 5 cups water
- 1 pack onion soup mix
- 3 sliced yellow onions

- 3 tablespoons butter
- 4 tablespoons flour
- 1 tablespoon soy sauce
- 2 bay leaves
- 1 can beer
- Oyster crackers (Vista Bakery)
- Grated Mozzarella cheese for taste

Bring water and water onion soup mix to a boil; simmer for about 10 minutes and set aside.

Brown onion into melted butter, stirring. Stir in flour,

reserved onion soup, soy sauce, bay leaves and beer; salt and pepper to taste.

Simmer for about 70 minutes. Pour into individual soup bowls; top with *__Vista Oyster Crackers__* and sprinkle with Mozzarella cheese.
Brown into a pre-heated oven at 450 degrees for about 5 minutes or until cheese is melted.

Go Green Bay!

Tim Brown's (Man I'm Busted) Beer Soup –

- 1 can beer
- 4 oz sugar
- 5 egg yolks
- 1 tablespoon garlic powder
- 1 chopped yellow onion

- 2 oz butter (Government issued if available)

Mix beer with yolks and sugar in a jar. Pour into a saucepan and beat with a whisk, until it boils. Add onion and garlic powder.

Remove from heat at boiling point, add butter and serve.

Note – Great with buttermilk biscuits!

Vince Moser's Pork Stew with Beer –

- 3 lb Pork boneless shoulder

- 1 tablespoon Olive oil
- 1 chopped yellow onion
- 3 Finely chopped garlic cloves
- 1 can whole tomatoes
- 1 finely chopped red chili pepper
- 3 tablespoons chopped cilantro
- 1 tea spoon salt
- 1 tablespoon dried oregano
- 1 can light beer
- 1 diced red pepper
- 1 pot hot cooked rice

Cut pork into 1-inch cubes. Heat oil in a Dutch oven until hot. Cook pork over medium heat, stirring frequently, until all liquid is evaporated and the pork is brown, about 30 minutes.

Remove with a slotted spoon. Drain all but 3 tablespoons fat from the pot. Cook and stir onion and garlic until all is tender.

(A seal walks into a bar. The bartender say's " what can I get ya?" The seal says " Anything but Canadian Club.")

Add tomatoes and heat to boiling. Reduce heat and simmer, uncovered for about 15 minutes.

Stir in pork and beer. Heat to boiling. Reduce heat. Cover and simmer for about 50 minutes. Stir in red pepper and reduce heat. Simmer, uncovered, until pork is tender and the sauce is thick.

Serve with the rice.

The Inebriation Scale

0- Stone cold sober. Brain as sharp as an army bayonet.

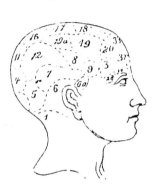

1- Still sober. Pleasure senses activated. Feeling of well – being.

2- Beer warming up head. Cheeseburgers are ordered. Barmaid complimented on choice of blouse.

3- Crossword in newspaper is filled in. After a while blanks are filled with random letters and numbers.

4- Barmaid complimented on choice of undergarments. Try to instigate conversation about undergarments. Pickled turkey gizzards are ordered.

5- Have brilliant discussion with a old guy at bar. Devise foolproof scheme for winning lottery, sort out problems with the N.F.L.

6- Feel like you did in college. Map out rest of life on beer mat. Realize that everybody loves you. Call up parents and tell them you love them.

7- Send drinks over to the chick sitting at table by dartboard. No reaction. Scribble out message of love on five beer mats and Frisbee them across the room. Chick gets mad. Receive first face slapping of the day.

8- Some slurring. Offer to buy drinks for everyone at the bar. Lots of people say yes. Go around the bar hugging them one by one. Fall over. Get up.

9- Headache kicks in. Beer tastes off. Send it back. Beer comes back tasting same. Say "that's much better". Fight nausea by trying to play poker machine for ten minutes before seeing "out of order" sign.

10- Some doubling of vision. Stand on table shouting abuse at all four bartenders. Talked down by bartenders' wives, whom you offer to give a baby to. Fall over. Get up. Fall over.

Impale head on corner of table. Fail to notice oozing head wound.

11-	Speech no longer possible. Eventually manage to find door. Sit and take stock. Realize you are sitting in bar cellar, having taken a wrong turn.

12-	Put in taxi by somebody. Give home

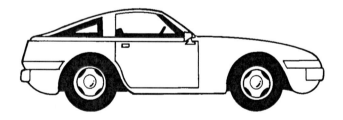

address. Taken home. Can't get key in door. Realize you've given address of local football club. Generally pleased at way evening has gone. Pass out again.

Steve Fenton's Beer, Cheese & Crawfish Soup

- 2 yellow onions, chopped
- 2 lbs crawfish tails
- 3 pints heavy cream
- 2 pints clam juice
- 2 quarts cheddar cheese sauce
- 2 tablespoons lobster base
- 1 tablespoon nutmeg
- 1 tablespoon white pepper
- 1 tablespoon garlic powder
- 1 teaspoon cayenne pepper
- 1 quart beer

In a large pan, sauté onions in butter. Add crawfish tails, cream, clam juice cheddar cheese sauce, and bring to a boil.

Add lobster base, nutmeg, white pepper, garlic powder, cayenne pepper, and beer.

Simmer on low heat for about 30 minutes.

Jeff May's Beer Cheese Soup –

- 1 cup chopped green onions
- 1 cup sliced celery
- 1 cup sliced carrots
- 10 ounces fresh mushrooms, sliced

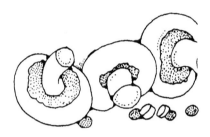

- ¾ cup butter
- ½ cup flour
- 1 teaspoon mustard powder
- 5 cups chicken broth
- 1 small head cauliflower
- 1 can beer
- 8 ounces sharp Cheddar cheese, shredded
- 3 tablespoons grated Parmesan cheese

Sauté green onions, celery, carrots, and mushrooms in butter. Mix flour and dry mustard into sautéed vegetables.
Add chicken broth, bring to boil.

Break up cauliflower into bite – size pieces, steam until tender.
Reduce heat of sautéed vegetables to a simmer; add cauliflower, beer, and cheeses.

Simmer for about 20 minutes. Add salt and pepper to taste.

Mike & April's Beer Soup -

- 6 cups beer
- 2 egg yolks
- 1 cup sour cream
- 1 teaspoon cornstarch
- 1 teaspoon white sugar
- ½ teaspoon salt
- 4 medium slices French bread, cut into 1 inch cubes
- 1 cup shredded Swiss cheese

In a medium saucepan over medium heat, bring beer, covered, to a boil.

Meanwhile, in a bowl, beat together egg yolks, sour cream, cornstarch, sugar and salt until well mixed. Transfer mixture to a large saucepan over low heat. Pour in hot beer, stirring until well combined. *Do not boil.*

To serve, divide bread cubes into four warmed soup bowls. Sprinkle cheese over bread.

Pour hot soup over all and serve.

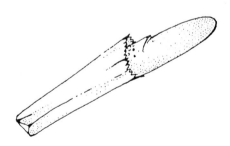

Some History on Brewski

As the cold golden liquid pours down your throat quenching your thirst, refreshing your body, and renewing your very spirit, have you ever wondered just what beer is? Why do we call it beer?

Well, one of these sheepskins apparently went bad and he ordered a "poison" sign placed on it until the sheepskin could be removed.

In the meantime, one of the chicks, trying to improve her position next to the Prince, framed the Prince's favorite chick.
The framed chick was thrown out of the harem.

Since the chick truly loved the Prince, she decided to kill herself in a fit of passion and, seeing the "poisonous" grapes, drank them down.

Since they were not poisonous, but merely fermented, the chick did not die but instead became rip-roaring drunk.

With her inhibitions gone, she slipped back into the harem and chopped off the head of her competition with a sword.
Her spirit impressed the Prince a great deal and that night he, too, tried the grape poison and liked the effect on himself and his chick.

The Prince ordered it served to all the chicks in his harem and thus began the time-honored tradition of getting chicks drunk.

From this tale, we get the famous bartender's query, *Name your poison.*

Now we all know that the grape juice was wine, therefore wine was the first alcoholic drink. But beer was the next!

And with this new information, I have just given you yet another subject to discuss while sitting at your local pub!

And you thought this was just a cookbook.

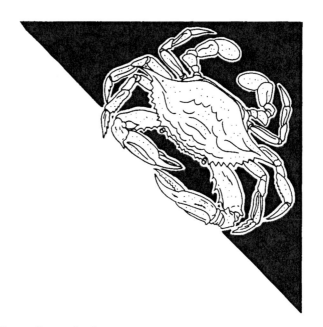

Seafood Cooked with Beer

Beer and seafood go together like Ted Nugent and a Les Paul guitar.
Ain't nothin' sweeter! Boys, I gotta tell ya, chicks dig a man who can cook up fish dripping in suds.
From beer batter to clams steamed in beer, I got just the recipes for you.

Think about it, all them dudes in Maine are making a lot of girly friends because they know how to cook up their harvest with beer.

Becky's Beer-Batter Tempura –

- ¾ cup beer
- ¾ cup flour
- 1 teaspoon salt
- 6 large shrimp, shelled
- 1 sweet potato
- 1 red pepper, cut into ¼ inch thick rings
- 6 asparagus spears, trimmed

In a large bowl whisk beer into flour until smooth and stir in salt.

Make several shallow cuts across inside curve of each shrimp.

Peel sweet potato and cut crosswise into ¼ inch slices.

In a 3-quart saucepan heat 2 inches of oil to 375 degrees. Working in batches of 3 pieces, dredge shrimp, sweet potato slices, bell pepper rings, and asparagus spears in batter to coat completely, letting excess drip off, and fry, turning, until golden brown, about 3 minutes.

After golden brown, place tempura on paper towels and serve with soy sauce.

Bubba's Mussels Steamed In Spiced Beer –

- 1 can beer
- 2 bay leaves
- 5 whole cloves
- 1 teaspoon coriander seeds
- 1 teaspoon mustard seeds
- 1 teaspoon cayenne pepper
- 1 teaspoon salt
- 2 lemon wedges
- 40 mussels, cultivated, scrubbed well in several changes of water and the beards scraped off.
- 3 tablespoons minced fresh parsley leaves for garnish

In a kettle bring the beer to a boil with the bay leaves, the cloves, coriander seeds, mustard seeds, cayenne pepper, salt, and the lemon wedges and boil the mixture, covered partially, for about 3 minutes.

Add the mussels; steam them, covered, over high heat, stirring them for about 10 minutes, or until they are opened.

Serve the mussels sprinkled with the parsley.

Beer – Battered Catfish On Vinegar Slaw –

- 1/3 cup plus 2 tablespoons flour
- 1 teaspoon salt
- 1 teaspoon black pepper
- 1/3 cup flat beer
- 2 catfish fillets
- 2 cups coleslaw mix
- 2 tablespoons white wine vinegar
- 1 ½ tablespoons honey
- Oil for cooking

Whisk 1/3-cup flour, salt, and pepper in a medium bowl to blend.
Whisk in beer.

Add about ½ inch oil in a large skillet. Heat oil to 350 degrees. Place remaining 2 tablespoons of flour on a plate.

Coat fish with flour. Dip in batter, letting excess drip off.
Fry fish until golden brown.
Drain fish on paper towels.

Toss coleslaw mix, vinegar, honey, and one-tablespoon oil in a bowl. Season with salt and pepper. Place fish atop of coleslaw.

Jennifer's Seafood Marinade –

- 1 can beer
- ¾ cup fresh lime juice
- 6 garlic cloves, minced
- 1 teaspoon chicken bouillon
- 1 tablespoon Worcestershire sauce
- 1 tablespoon black pepper
- 1 yellow onion, chopped very fine

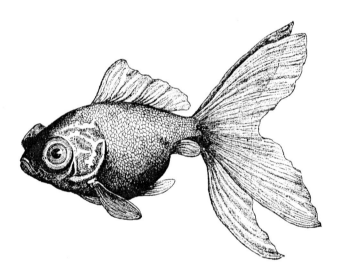

Whisk all ingredients in a bowl to blend. Let marinade stand for about an hour before using. This marinade will last about a week, covered in the refrigerator.

Note, this is a great marinade for any fish. Start marinating at least 30 minutes before grilling.

Shaena's Fried Fish Tacos –

- 1 quart cooking oil
- 16 corn tortillas
- 1 cup flour
- 2 tablespoons salt
- 1 tablespoon garlic powder
- 1 cup beer
- 1 pound cod fillet, cut into 1 inch strips

Accompaniments: Shredded lettuce, sour cream, avocado slices, chopped radish, red salsa, and lime wedges.

Heat 1- inch oil in a heavy pot until 360 degrees. Meanwhile, separate tortillas and make 2 stacks of 8. Wrap each stack in foil and heat in oven for about 15 minutes.

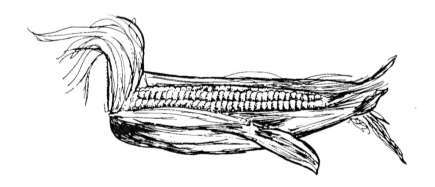

While tortillas warm, stir together flour and salt in a large bowl, and then stir in beer.

Gently stir fish into batter to coat.
Lift each piece of fish out of batter, wiping any excess off.

Fry the fish in batches, turning until golden brown. Drain on paper towels.

Assemble tacos with the warm tortillas, fish and accompaniments.

This is a great tasting dish. So try it! You'll like it!

Shanea says so.

Beer Trivia!

- Seven percent of the entire Irish barley crop goes to the production of Guinness beer!

- Ancient Egyptians recommended mixing half an onion with beer foam as a way of warding death.

- The first beer brewed in England was made by Picts about 250 B.C. The beverage was made from heather and may have had hallucinogenic properties.

- In medieval England, beer was often served with breakfast.

- Beer wasn't sold in bottles until 1850. Before then, a person went to the local tavern with a special beer bucket to have it filled.

- The Pilgrims landed at Plymouth Rock because of beer. The Mayflower's logbook shows the crew didn't want to waste beer by looking for another site.

- Britain is only ranked 7th in world beer consumption. The average Brit will drink 180 pints a year. The heaviest beer drinkers are the Czech Republic, who drinks on an average of 285 pints.

- Of all the major brewing nations, England remains the only one in which ale is the primary beer consumed. This in contrast to lager, which is the world's overall dominant beer of choice.

- If we were to up-turn the Millennium Dome it would take 2 billion liters of beer to fill it up.

- A Labeorphilist is a collector of beer bottles.

- Declaring that he was an alcoholic, Ozzy Osbourne quit performing and opened a bar. He soon drank up all his stock and wasted his money until he rejoined his band.

- In 1116 BC Chinese imperial edict claimed that the use of beer in moderation was required by heaven.

- The word "groggy" originally referred to a person who was drunk on "grog"...Grog being beer!

- A dyslexic man walks into a bra.

Caper Beer Batter in Scallion, Broccoli & Carrots. Deep Fried –

- 1 ½ cups flour
- 1 can beer
- 8 scallions, chopped fine
- 2 tablespoons drained bottled capers, chopped fine
- 2 tablespoons salt
- 1 head broccoli, cut into bite size chunks
- 4 carrots, diced

Preheat the oven to 325 degrees. In a large bowl whisk together the flour, beer, scallions, capers, and the salt.

In a heavy pot heat 1 ½ inches of oil to 375 degrees. When heat is reached, dip the broccoli in the batter, and fry until golden brown.

Continue the same method for the remaining ingredients.

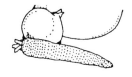

This dish is great with fried potatoes, cooked in the left over oil.

Sgt. Roy's Steamers In Beer –

- 2 pounds soft – shelled clams, less than 2 inches in diameter.
- 1 shallot
- ¼ cup butter
- 1 cup beer
- 1 tablespoon finely chopped parsley
- 1 teaspoon slat

Clean clams well. Finely chop shallot. In a large saucepan cook the shallot in butter.

Add beer and clams, steam clams, covered for about 10 minutes. Transferring then to a bowl as soon as done.

Pour reserved cooking liquid into a saucepan. Heat cooking liquid over medium heat until hot.

This dish is great served with sweet corn and potatoes diced in butter.

John's Fast Shrimp & Beer Stew –

5 pounds shrimp (uncooked from dealer)
4 tablespoons butter
2 quarts of beer
2 white onions, chopped
5 tablespoons garlic powder
2 tablespoons black pepper
2 tablespoons salt
1 cup milk
2 tablespoons cayenne pepper

In a large pan cook shrimp for about 5 minutes in boiling water,
Drain shrimp and remove shrimp from shell.
Save water from boiling shrimp. Add the remaining ingredients and return to a boil for about 2 minutes.

Remove and strain all ingredients from pot, then place back into pot on low heat for about 30 minutes.

This dish is great with cornbread and butter!

Burlington Beer Batter Fried Sardines –

- 1 cup beer
- 1 teaspoon salt
- ¾ cup flour
- 3 cans of sardines
- 1 lime
- 4 cups oil
- 1 white pepper

In a large bowl whisk beer, salt, and pepper into flour until smooth.
Drain sardines and pat dry with a paper towel. Cut lime into about 8 wedges.

In a large saucepan heat oil to 375 degrees. Dredge the sardines in batter to coat completely.
Fry about 5 sardines in a batch for about 3 minutes or until golden brown.

Place the fried sardines on a paper towel to drain.
Fry the lime wedges until they turn golden brown.

Serve fish with the lime.

Darren's Beer Baked Trout –

- 1 can beer (dark)
- 6 trout fillets
- 6 red potatoes, chopped in halves
- 1 yellow onion, finely chopped
- 1 lemon, cut in wedges
- 1 lime, cut in wedges
- 1 tablespoon garlic salt
- 1 tablespoon white pepper
- 2 tablespoons olive oil

Pre-heat oven to 350 degrees. In a large baking pan add the beer, fish, potatoes, onion, lemon, lime, garlic salt, pepper, and olive oil.

Bake dish uncovered for about 30 minutes. Reduce heat to 200 degrees, cover dish with foil and bake on low for about 10 minutes, or until the potatoes are done.

Serve fish with the potatoes covered with the juices from the baking dish.

- Four fonts walk into a bar. The bar tender says "get out, we don't want your type in here!"

- Two peanuts walk into a bar, one is salted.

- A sandwich walks into a bar. The bar tender says "sorry we don't serve food here."

- A priest, and a rabbi walk into a bar. The bartender says " is this some kind of joke?"

- Darren walks into a bar and tells the bartender to line up 10 glasses and start filling them with beer. So the bartender starts filling the glasses up with beer, and Darren is right behind him drinking them straight down. The bartender says, "Hey buddy what's your hurry?" Darren says if you had what I have you would do the same thing. The bartender backs up and says "what do you have?" Darren says about 75 cents.

Jimmy's Chicken Beer Fried Rice –

- 2 cups uncooked white rice
- 1 tablespoon butter
- 2 skinless, boneless, chicken breast halves, cubed
- ½ cup beer
- 2 eggs beaten
- 1 cup sliced mushrooms
- 2 green onions, chopped
- 1 tablespoon soy sauce

In a large saucepan bring 3 ½ cups water and beer to a boil. Add rice and stir.
Reduce heat, cover and simmer for about 20 minutes.

Heat butter in a large skillet over medium heat. Brown chicken in butter and set aside.
Transfer cooked rice to the skillet that the chicken was cooked in, stirring to brown.

In a separate skillet, scramble eggs.
Add the chicken, mushrooms, green onions, eggs, and soy sauce to the rice.

Chicken Cooked With Beer

In this section we explore the art of cooking chicken with beer. Not as fun as seafood, but just the same. And my publisher wants me to have recipes for everyone to use, not just for wild men like me!

I know this is kind of a funny lookin' chicken but this is how our chickens look ever since they built that new nuke plant up river.

So here are some sissy dishes using chicken. Wait! I forgot! These meals will be cooked with beer!
Any meal cooked with beer cant be a sissy thing!
COOL! Cancel my first statements and let's move on to the manly art of cooking chicken with beer!

Hawkeye's Beer Chicken -

- 4 skinless, boneless chicken breast halves
- 5 ounces Dijon mustard
- ½ cup teriyaki sauce
- ½ cup beer
- ½ cup bacon bits
- ½ cup Parmesan cheese

Preheat oven to 400 degrees. Place chicken in a baking dish.
Cover chicken with mustard, then pour beer and teriyaki sauce over all.
Sprinkle with bacon bits, then cover with cheese.

Bake at 400 degrees for about 35 minutes.

Dean & Stephanie's Beer & Garlic Chicken –

- 1 can beer
- 3 tablespoons butter
- 4 skinless, boneless chicken breast halves
- 2 teaspoons garlic powder
- 1 teaspoon seasoning salt
- 3 tablespoons minced onion
- 1 tablespoon onion powder

Marinate chicken with beer and minced onion overnight in the refrigerator.

When ready to cook, melt butter in a large skillet over medium heat.
Add marinated chicken and sprinkle with garlic powder, seasoned salt, and onion powder.

Sauté about 20 minutes on each side, or until chicken is fully cooked and brown.

Now Mr. Fields can get pretty ornery from time to time, so I highly recommend that if you invited to eat some of Stephanie's home cook 'in, I would bring a bottle of good Scotch. Just to be on the safe side!

Just kidding Boss!

Bill & Mary's Pontoon –Beer & Chicken –

- 2 skinless, boneless chicken breast, cut into bite size chunks.
- 1 tablespoon chili powder
- 2 tablespoons olive oil
- 1 cup chopped green bell pepper
- ½ cup beer
- ½ cup chopped yellow onion
- 2 jalapeno peppers, seeded and minced
- 1 tomato diced
- 1 tablespoon hot sauce

Season chicken with salt and pepper. Heat oil in a large skillet over medium heat and sauté chicken for about 5 minutes.

Remove the chicken from skillet when done. In the same skillet, add bell peppers, onions, jalapeno peppers, tomatoes, beer, Chile powder and hot sauce.

Stir fry for about 8 minutes; add cooked chicken and cook for about 3 more minutes

Now if you don't have the money for a good bottle of Scotch to take to the Fields, I know where Bill keeps his on his boat! Information can be bought!

Jim & Mary's Brown Rice & Beer Chicken –

- 1 tablespoon olive oil
- 4 boneless chicken breast
- 1 tablespoon garlic powder
- 1 teaspoon dried rosemary
- 1 can chicken broth
- ½ cup beer (flat)
- 1 cup brown rice, uncooked

Heat oil in a large skillet on medium heat. Season chicken with salt and pepper and add to skillet.

Cook chicken for about 5 minutes on each side and remove from skillet when cooked.

Add broth and beer to the same skillet and bring to a boil while stirring.
Stir in rice, garlic powder, and rosemary. Top with cooked chicken; cover and cook on low heat for about 10 minutes or until rice is fully cooked.

Now I would pick on Jim, but Mary can kick my butt!

25 Reasons Why Beer Is Better Than Woman
(Boys, don't try these at home)

1. You don't have to wine and dine a beer.
2. Your beer will always wait patiently for you in the car.
3. When beer goes flat you toss it out.
4. Beer is never late.

5. Hangovers eventually go away.
6. A beer doesn't get jealous when you grab another beer.
7. Beer labels come off without a fight.
8. When you go to the bar, you know you can always pick up a beer.
9. Beer never has a headache.
10. A beer won't get upset if you come home with beer on your breath.
11. You can have more than one beer a night and not feel guilty.
12. A beer always goes down gently.
13. You can share a beer with your buddies.
14. You always know that you are the first one to pop a beer.

15. A beer doesn't care when you come home.
16. You can have a beer in public.
17. A frigid beer is a good beer.
18. After you have a beer, you're committed to nothing other than dumping the empty bottle.
19. A beer never costs you more than five dollars and never leaves you thirsty.
20. When your beer is gone, you just pop another.

Erma & Marvin's Chicken & Beer Dumplings

3 slices bacon
3 potatoes, peeled and diced
1 yellow onion, diced
4 chicken breast, diced
2 ½ cups chicken broth
½ cup beer (lite)

1 tablespoon seasoned salt
1 can corn, drained
3 cups half and half
1 ½ cups biscuit mix
1 cup milk

Place bacon in a large skillet and cook until crisp.
Drain, crumble and set aside, keeping the bacon
drippings in the skillet

Add the potatoes, onion, and chicken to bacon drippings
and sauté for about 20 minutes, stirring occasionally.

Pour in chicken broth, beer, seasoned salt, and black
pepper. Stir in corn and simmer for about 20 minutes.

Pour in half and half and bring to a boil, add the bacon.
In a bowl, combine biscuit mix with milk and mix. Drop
tablespoon sizes of dough into boiling mixture, reduce
heat and simmer for 10 minutes uncovered, then another
10 minutes covered.

The dough will be thick. Do not stir while simmering.

Kim & Kalian's Chicken Beer Meat –

- 3 tablespoons olive oil
- 2 pounds ground chicken (or turkey)
- 1 green bell pepper, chopped
- 4 garlic cloves, chopped
- 3 tablespoons chili powder
- 1 ½ cups beer
- 1 cup ketchup
- 1 can green chilies
- 3 tablespoons Worcestershire sauce
- 1 cup green onions, chopped

Heat oil in a large saucepan; add chicken, green pepper, and garlic sauté for about 15 minutes or until chicken is tender.

Mix in chili powder and all remaining ingredients. Cook on low heat for about 20 minutes.

Serve with your favorite bread.

Grandma Black's Braised Chicken Necks –

- 10 chicken necks
- 10 tablespoons oil
- 2 onions, chopped

- 2 carrots, chopped
- 2 cloves garlic, chopped
- 10 tablespoons tomato puree
- ½ can beer
- 1 cup water
- 5 tablespoons flour
- 12 tablespoons parsley, chopped

Fry necks in oil until brown, then remove and place them in a large casserole dish. Sauté the vegetables in the same skillet and place with chicken in casserole dish.

Add flour to the skillet that the chicken and veggies were cooked in and add beer and water, whisking until smooth. Add tomato puree and cook on low for about 20 minutes.

Pour the sauce from the skillet over the chicken and veggies and bake at 400 degrees for about 1 hour.

21. You rarely (if ever) find beer labels on the shower curtain rod.
22. Beer looks the same in the morning.
23. Beer doesn't look you up in a month.
24. Beer doesn't worry about someone walking in.

25. Beer doesn't have a mother!!!!!!

Stanfield's Baked Beer Basted Chicken –

- 1 large whole chicken
- 1 can beer
- 8 green onions, chopped
- ½ cup soy sauce
- ¼ cup lemon juice
- 3 tablespoons brown sugar
- 2 tablespoons ginger, ground
- 2 tablespoons garlic, chopped
- 1 tablespoon sesame oil

Combine all ingredients in a large resealed plastic bag. Refrigerate over night.

Pre-heat oven to 350 degrees. Place chicken and marinade in a large baking pan.
Roast chicken for about 1-½ hours.

Transfer chicken to platter. Pour juices into a saucepan and boil to reduce and thicken.
Serve with sauce.

Beef Cooked With Beer

Man, the opportunities on cooking food with beer are mind-boggling! There just isn't enough time in the day to write them all out. Hum, This may call for yet another book!
Well in any case, I have found 10 of my favorite beef and suds recipes for your cooking pleasure.

Kinnick Liver & Onions –

- 1 cup flour
- 2 teaspoons salt
- 1 teaspoon black pepper
- 8 -½ inch –thick slices calf's' liver
- 3 tablespoons oil
- 1 tablespoon butter
- ½ cup beer
- 2 pounds onions, sliced

Combine flour, salt, and pepper in a bowl. Coat liver with seasoned flour, shaking off excess.

Heat oil in a large skillet over medium heat. Sauté liver until fully cooked. Transfer to warming plate.

Melt butter in same skillet, add beer and bring to a boil, scraping up browned bits.
Add onions, simmer until tender, and season with salt and pepper.

Smother onions over cooked liver.

Becky's Beef in Beer –

- 2 pounds chuck roast, cut into 8 slices
- 2 tablespoons butter
- 2 tablespoons oil
- 6 onions, sliced
- 2 tablespoons flour
- 2 cups beer (dark)
- 1 teaspoon thyme, dried
- 1 bay leaf, chopped
- 1 teaspoon salt
- 1 teaspoon black pepper

Season beef with salt and pepper. In a heavy pan, melt butter and oil.

Brown the meat in butter and oil on high heat and remove. Add onions and cook slowly until soft, stirring frequently. Add the flour and stir to blend.
Keep stirring over medium heat until flour begins to brown.

Pour in the beer and stir until thickened and simmering. Return the beef to the pan and add thyme and bay leaf. Cover and cook on low heat for about 3 hours. Add more beer during cooing if needed.

Bubba's Beer Burgers –

- 3 pounds lean ground beef
- 1 packet dry onion soup mix
- ¼ cup beer (dark)
- 1 tablespoon garlic powder
- ¼ teaspoon cayenne pepper
- 1 tablespoon Worcestershire sauce

In a large bowl, combine all ingredients together and cover bowl with plastic wrap.

Place bowl in the refrigerator for 2 hours. Fire up the grill and grill burgers until cooked the way you like them.

Great with Right-A-Way Ranch Beer beans (recipe coming up)

Mississippi River Pirate Plate –

- 2 pounds ground beef
- 1 yellow onion, chopped
- ½ cup cheddar cheese, grated
- 1 cup tomato soup
- 2 stalks celery, chopped
- 4 cups cooked macaroni
- 1 tablespoon garlic powder
- 1 teaspoon, ground ginger
- 1 cup beer

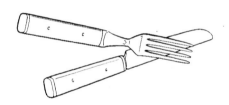

In a large skillet brown ground beef and drain. Add all remaining ingredients other than cheese and simmer for about 30 minutes.

After simmering, top with cheese. Serve with garlic toast and of course, BEER!!

Paris Island Steak –

- 2 large sirloin steaks
- 2 cans beer
- ½ cup olive oil
- 1 tablespoon wine vinegar
- 2 tablespoons onion powder
- 2 tablespoons minced garlic
- 1 tablespoon soy sauce

Mix together the beer, oil, vinegar, onion powder, minced garlic, and soy sauce.

Marinate the steaks in mixture for about an hour. Grill steaks until tender or to your liking.

Bubba's Beer Drinking Rules
(You are officially cut off if you break these rules)

1. No Dual – Openers – Anyone accidentally opening another beer, before finishing their current beer, is cut off.
2. No Spillage – Spilling any amount of beer will get you cut off and thrown out! You better come up with one hell of an excuse to get out of this one.

3. No Ghosting – Forgetting where you left your beer is only forgiven if you don't break the "5 second rule." Remember where it is in 5 seconds or less and you may continue to indulge.
4. No Freeloading – You may show up once without bringing your own supply. After that, you are cut off!
5. No Carousing – Under no circumstances may you hit on your bud's spouse, UNLESS you bud says it's okay!

6. No Warm Brew – Bringing warm (non refrigerated) beer deserves a beating.
7. No Hyper-Pumpers – Take it easy on the keg, you only have to pump it once or twice while the tap is OPEN - - get it?

8. No Pretenders – You either can or can't handle your beer ––'nuff said.
9. No Opps! – An opp's is what most of us say when we open the freezer and discover that we left beer in too long! We've all done it, but three opp's and you're outta here!
10. No Butting – Accidentally or purposely dropping a cigarette butt into an otherwise good beer will get you thrown out and chastised until the end of time!
11. No Mine Sweeping – There is no excuse for losing track of your beer and grabbing the closest beer as if it were yours. Get your own.
12. No Dead Soldiers – No passing out before first finishing your beer!

Beer Glazed Burger & Onions –

- 4 quarter pound patties, burger
- 4 tablespoons olive oil
- 4 yellow onions, sliced ¼ inch thick
- 1 teaspoon salt
- 1 teaspoon white pepper
- ¼ teaspoon cayenne pepper
- ¼ cup beer (dark)

In a large skillet on medium heat, add onions, salt, pepper, and cayenne stirring constantly.

Continue cooking until onions reach a golden caramel color.
Poor in the beer and cook for about 5 more minutes.
Meanwhile, grill the burgers and when finished, top with the glazed onions.

25 More Reasons why Beer is Better Than Woman!
Hey don't blame me, you asked for it!

1. Beer doesn't have morals.
2. Beer doesn't go crazy once a month.
3. Beer always listens and never argues.
4. Beer labels don't go out of style every year.
5. Beer doesn't whine, it bubbles.
6. Beer doesn't have cold hands and feet.
7. Beer is never overweight.
8. If you change beers, you don't have to pay alimony.
9. Beer won't run off with your credit cards.
10. Beer doesn't have a lawyer.
11. Beer doesn't need much closet space.
12. Beer doesn't complain about the way you drive.
13. Beer doesn't mind if you belch out loudly.
14. Beer never changes its mind.
15. Beer doesn't play hard to get.
16. Beer never asks you to change the station.
17. Beer doesn't make you go to the mall.
18. Beer doesn't tell you how to mow the grass.
19. Beer will never make you go to a love story movie.
20. Beer is always easy to pick up.

21. Big, fat beers are nice to have.
22. Beer doesn't pout.
23. Beer never says no.
24. Beer doesn't need to go to the "powder room" with other beers.

25. Beer doesn't live with its mother!

Spanky's Drunken Deviled Beer Burgers –

- 1 pound ground beef
- 1 teaspoon salt
- 1 teaspoon pepper
- 1 teaspoon yellow mustard
- 1 teaspoon Worcestershire sauce
- 2 teaspoons horseradish
- 4 teaspoons catsup
- ¼ cup beer

Combine all ingredients together and mix well. Make into ¼ pound patties and broil. Serve with chips and coleslaw.

Whiskey Eyed Eddie's Roast –

- 1 large rump roast
- 1 tablespoon seasoned salt
- ¼ cup flour
- 1 teaspoon thyme
- 1 clove garlic, crushed
- 1 cup beer
- 1 tablespoon olive oil
- 1 teaspoon white pepper
- 2 tablespoons dried marjoram
- 2 tablespoons dried rosemary
- 1 cup apple juice

Cut several slits in roast about ½ inch deep. Rub roast with oil, sprinkle with salt and pepper.

Combine the next five ingredients; pat mixture on roast and stuff into the slits.

Pour apple juice and beer into a shallow baking pan. Put roast in and bake uncovered in preheated 325-degree oven for about an hour, basting often.

Creamed Beer Sauce with Beef & Noodles –

- 8 ounces noodles, cooked
- 1 pound ground beef
- 1 yellow onion, diced
- 1 teaspoon dill weed
- 1 can cream of mushroom soup
- ½ cup sour cream
- ¼ cup beer

Prepare noodles as label directs. Meanwhile, in a skillet over medium heat, cook beef, onions, and dill until meat is browned, drain.

Stir in undiluted soup, sour cream, beer, salt and pepper; cook until heated through.
Serve over hot noodles.

Beef & Beer Tenderloin Sandwiches –

- 2 yellow onions, sliced
- 2 cans sliced mushrooms, drained
- ¼ cup butter
- ¼ cup Worcestershire sauce
- ¼ cup beer (dark)
- 8 beef tenderloin steaks
- 1 tablespoon garlic powder
- 1 teaspoon white pepper
- 1 teaspoon salt
- 4 hard rolls, split

In a large skillet, sauté the onions and mushrooms in butter, beer, and Worcestershire sauce until onions are tender.
Add steaks to the skillet and cook over medium heat for about 3 minutes on each side.

Sprinkle with garlic powder, salt, and pepper. Place two steaks on each roll; top with onions and mushrooms.

Rick's Reasons why beer should be served at work!

- It's an incentive to show up.

- It reduces stress.

- Sitting on the copy machine will no longer be seen as "gross."

- It leads to more honest communications.

- It reduces complaints about low pay.

- It cuts down on time off because you can work with a hangover.

- Employees tell management what they think, not what management wants to hear.

- It helps save on heating costs in the winter.

- It encourages carpooling.

- Increase job satisfaction because if you have a bad job, you don't care.

- It eliminates vacations because people would rather come to work.

- It makes fellow employees look better.

- It makes the cafeteria food taste better.

- Bosses are more likely to hand out raises when they are wasted.

- Salary negotiations are a lot more profitable.

- Suddenly, burping during a meeting isn't so embarrassing.

- Employees work later since there's no longer a need to relax at the bar.

- It makes everyone more open with his ideas.
- Everyone agrees the work is better after they've had a couple of beers.

- Eliminates the need for employees to get drunk on their lunch break.

- Increases the chance of seeing your boss naked.(?)

- The janitor's closet will finally have a use.

- Employees no longer need coffee to sober up.

- Babbling and mumbling incoherently will be common language.

Pork Cooked With Beer

Ok we have covered soups & Stews, Seafood, Chicken, and Beef. Now we come to Pork "the other white meat".

Now my claim to fame is wild game cooking, however, so far, I'm having fun with this, keeping in mind that my favorite part of this book is coming up. Mountain Man Cooking! Oh yea. So kick back, settle down, and read every page. Heck who knows, you just might let out a giggle.

Cancel the giggle.....Real men don't giggle!

Bratwurst Braised in Beer & Apples –

    4 cans beer
    1 yellow onion, sliced
    2 Granny Smith apples, peeled, sliced
    6 of your favorite bratwurst

Bring beer, onion and apples to a simmer. Add sausages and cook for 5 minutes.

Remove sausages from the beer, onion and apple mixture. Grill sausages until golden brown (3-5 minutes) When sausages are done place the cooked beer mix back on the sausages. This mix now serves as a sauce.

<u>Dale's Pork Loin Cooked in Beer –</u>

- 3 pounds pork loin roast
- 2 tablespoons oil
- 1 tablespoon salt
- 1 tablespoon white pepper
- 1 teaspoon garlic powder
- 2 cup beer

Brown the meat on all sides in the oil on medium heat. Season the pork with salt, pepper, and garlic powder.

Add beer and simmer for about and hour, or until tender when pierced with a fork.
Stir the dish from time to time to avoid the roast sticking to the pan.

Remove the pork roast, slice and cover with the sauce to serve.

Old Nauvoo "Mormon Trail Style" Sandwich-

- 10 pound boneless pork butt, trimmed of fat
- 5 tablespoons olive oil
- 1 yellow onion, diced
- 7 garlic cloves, minced
- ¼ cup paprika
- 3 tablespoons thyme
- 2 tablespoons oregano
- 2 tablespoons black pepper
- 2 tablespoons salt
- 2 cups beer
- 4 cups barbecue sauce (Your favorite)
- 25 hamburger buns

Remove any fat or bone from the pork and cut into 1" cubes.

In a large skillet, place pork cubes, onions, garlic cloves, paprika, thyme, oregano, salt, and pepper.

Fry for 30 minutes. Then place into a 350-degree oven for 30 minutes.

Add beer, cover, and bake at 300 degrees for about two hours.

When done, set out at wagon temperature (room) for about an hour.

When meat is cool, drain any excess juices and shred with a large fork.

Stir in BBQ sauce and season to taste with salt and pepper.

Serve the BBQ pork on toasted buns.

Old Squaw Chops & Mushrooms -

- 2 large, thick cut pork chops
- 1 can mushrooms
- 1 teaspoon garlic salt
- 1 tablespoon parsley
- 1 can beer (dark)

In a large skillet. Sear each side of chops to seal in the juices.
Add beer and bring to boil. Add mushrooms, garlic salt, and parsley.

Cook chops on medium heat until beer is close to boiling off.
Serve with salad.

T-Bone's, Ham in Bone Cooked in Beer –

- 1 large ham (15-20 pound)
- 1 can sliced pineapple
- 2 can beer
- ½ cup 7UP soda

Preheat oven to 325 degrees. Grease a large roasting pan. Place ham, with fattier side up, in the roaster.
Use toothpicks to secure pineapple rings on ham.

Pour beer over ham and add soda pop, cover roasting pan and bake for about 8 hours.
Remove the pineapple rings and let sit for 15 minutes before slicing.

THE OFFICIAL BEER BUDDY "CODE OF CONDUCT"

- Thou shale not rent the movie Chocolat.

- Under no circumstances may 2 men share an umbrella.

- Unless he murdered someone in your immediate family, you must bail a buddy out of jail within 12 hours.

- You may exaggerate any anecdote told in a bar by 50 percent without recrimination; beyond that, anyone within earshot is allowable to call "BULL!" (Exception" –

When trying to pick up a chick, the allowable exaggeration rate rises to 400 percent.

- If you've known a guy for more than 24 hours, his sister is off-limits forever.

- The maximum amount of time you have to wait for another guy who's running late is 5 minutes. For a chick, you are required to wait 10 minutes for every point of hotness she scores on the classic 1-10 scale.

- Complaining or "dogging out" about the brand of free beer in a buddy's refrigerator is forbidden. You may gripe if the temperature is unsuitable.

- No man is ever required to buy a birthday present for another man. In fact, even remembering a buddy's birthday is strictly optional. Except if buddy knows hot chicks and annually throws a birthday bash.

- Agreeing to distract the ugly friend of a hot chick your buddy is trying to hook up with is your legal duty. Sorry it's the law.

- Before dating a buddy's ex, you are required to ask his permission and he, in return, is required to grant it.

- Women who claim they "love to watch sports" must be treated as spies until they demonstrate knowledge of the game and, more importantly, the ability to pick a hot buffalo wing clean. <u>"Kris Wilke, Burlington Iowa, Is such a chick!" Boys don't pick on her Steelers!</u>

- If a man's zipper is down, that's his problem-you didn't see nothin'.

- The universal compensation for buddies who help you move .....is beer.

- If a buddy is already singing along to a song in the car, you may not join him......Think about it.... Does the word SISSY chime in?

- It is permissible to consume a fruity drink only when you're sunning on a tropical beach, and a topless chick delivers it, and it's free.

- If a buddy is outnumbered, out manned, or too drunk to fight, you must jump into the fight. Exception: If within the last 24 hours his actions have caused you to think, "What this guy needs is a good whooping", then you may set back and enjoy.

- A buddy in the company of a hot, suggestively dressed chick must remain sober enough to fight.

- Never hesitate to reach for the last beer or the last slice of pizza, but not both. That's just plain mean.

<u>Hayman's Salty Balls</u> — *Man, I could have had fun with this! But unless this book reaches sales of over a million copies, I still need my job. However, Old man Crandall across the river can still take a few good shots at Bill!*

- 2 pounds ground ham
- 2 pounds ground beef
- 2 cups graham crackers
- 1 cup milk
- ½ cup beer (dark)
- 3 eggs
- 1 can tomato soup

- ½ cup vinegar
- ½ brown sugar
- 3 tablespoons dry mustard

Preheat oven to 350 degrees. In a large bowl mix together the ham, beef, crackers, milk, beer, and eggs.

Roll mixture into 2-inch balls and place in a large baking pan. In another bowl, mix together the soup, vinegar, sugar, and mustard. Cover the balls with sauce and bake for about an hour.

Five Finger Freddy's "Crandall Alamode" –

- 1 cup rice
- 8 slices of wheat bread (torn up)

- 1 can cream of mushroom soup
- 1 can chicken rice soup
- 1 can mushrooms
- 2 pounds ground pork
- ½ cup beer (dark)
- 1 can cream of celery soup
- 1 yellow onion, diced
- 1 tablespoon garlic salt
- 2 cups cheddar cheese, shredded

Preheat oven to 325 degrees. In a large skillet brown the pork.
Cook the rice as directed on the package.
Mix all the first 10 ingredients together and place in a large greased casserole dish.

Top off dish with the cheese and bake for about 45 minutes.

Rock & Roll Beer Chops –

- 6 boneless pork chops
- 2 cans cream of mushroom soup
- 6 potatoes, peeled and sliced
- 1 can lima beans, drained

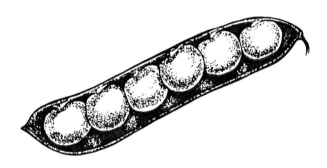

- 1 can mushrooms, drained
- ½ cup beer
- 1 yellow onion, chopped

In a large skillet, brown the chops and remove when finished.

Mix together the remaining ingredients and return the mixture with the chops back to the skillet.
Simmer on low heat until the potatoes are tender. Salt and pepper to taste.

It's Good To Be A Man "Coolash" –

- 8 cups cooked macaroni
- 1 can whole tomatoes
- 2 pounds sausage, ground
- 1 can vegetable juice

- 2 yellow onions, chopped
- 1 green pepper, chopped
- ½ cup beer
- ½ cup bacon bits
- 3 tablespoons garlic powder

In a large pot brown and drain sausage. Add onions and green pepper to pot and cook on low heat until they are tender.

Add the remaining ingredients to pot and cook on low heat for about 30 minutes.

Billy's Beer BLT"s –

- 2 pounds bacon
- ¼ cup beer
- 1 yellow onion, sliced
- Lettuce
- Tomatoes, sliced

In a large skillet brown bacon and drain fat from skillet. Add beer and onions to skillet with bacon and simmer until beer is boiled away.

Add bacon to your favorite bread with the lettuce and tomatoes.

Mountain Man Cooking

Born to be wild! Boys, ain't no one meaner than a drunken buck skinner with an empty belly. Of the great time I have had writing this book, this is the chapter I had been waiting for.

If you're a Rick Black groupie, then you know I love writing about wild game and hunting. So it only makes darn good sense that I get all crazy eyed over writing about cookin stuff up with such things as tree rat (Squirrel) and beaver (The four legged type).

So get a good one and get ready for some cool eatin!

I dig this so much, I think I will do a whole book on

Mountain Man Cooking!

Mizer's Bear Roast –

I told you this stuff was cool!

- 3 pounds boneless bear roast
- 2 onions, chopped
- ½ cup beer
- 3 clove garlic, minced
- 1 orange, peeled and sectioned
- ½ cup orange juice
- ½ cup celery, chopped
- 3 tablespoons pork fat (bacon grease)

Preheat oven to 400 degrees. In a large Dutch oven place pork fat, onion, celery, garlic, orange slices, and meat.

Combine all liquids and pour over meat. Cover and bake for about 2 hours, checking and basting every ½ hour.

Fried Skunk –

- 3 skunks, skinned
- 2 tablespoons salt
- 2 cups oil
- 3 egg yolks, beaten
- 2 cups milk
- Beer to cover meat
- 2 cups flour
- 2 tablespoons baking powder
- 2 tablespoons garlic powder

Cut skunks up into small serving pieces. Place meat in a large pot and cover with beer and bring to a boil.
Cook meat for about 40 minutes.

Remove all scum that rises to the surface. Make batter by mixing together the egg, milk, flour, salt, garlic powder, and baking powder.

Heat oil in a large fryer, dip the pieces of skunk in batter, and fry them until golden brown.
Taste just like chicken!

She been with the buck's Turtle Stew –

- 3 pounds turtle, cut in one inch chunks
- ½ cup pork fat (bacon grease)
- 2 yellow onions, chopped
- 2 cups celery, chopped
- 1 can lima beans, drained
- 8 potatoes, peeled and diced
- 1 cup beer

In a large skillet, brown meat in fat until golden on all sides.
In a large pot, add onions, celery, beans, potatoes, beer, and water to cover ingredients.

Bring mixture to a boil. After boiling, lower heat and simmer for about an hour. Add beer and meat and simmer for another hour.

Becky's Beaver – ???

I only do this to ....Well, I guess I will never learn!

- 1 large beaver striped of fat – *I'm in so much trouble!*

- 1 cup onions, diced
- 1 cup carrots, diced
- 1 cup beer

Preheat oven to degrees. Season meat with salt and pepper and put meat in a Dutch oven.

Add onions, carrots, and beer. Cover and bake for about 2 hours checking and basting every 30 minutes. This will make the beaver moist. *That's it; I'm a dead man!*

Tree Rat "Camp fire style" –

- 3 large squirrels, skinned and cleaned
- 3 yellow onions, peeled
- Beer to cover meat
- 1 camp fire (outside, not in your kitchen)

In a large pot, add meat, onions, and cover with beer. Boil meat in beer for about 30 minutes.

Remove meat and let cool then place on cooking sticks and cook over fire until browned. Peel off meat and enjoy! Great with Right –Away – Ranch beans!

Beer Troubleshooting

Symptom: Feet cold and wet.
Fault: Glass being held at incorrect angle.
Action: Rotate glass so that open end points toward ceiling.

Symptom: Feet warm and wet.
Fault: Improper bladder control.
Action: Stand next to nearest dog, complain about house training.

Symptom: Beer unusually pale and tasteless.
Fault: Glass empty.
Action: Get buddy to buy you another beer.

Symptom: Opposite wall covered with fluorescent lights.
Fault: You have fallen over backward.
Action: Have yourself leashed to bar.

Symptom: Mouth contains cigarette butts.
Fault: You have fallen forward.
Action: See above.

Symptom: Beer tasteless. Front of your shirt is wet.
Fault: Mouth not open, or glass applied to wrong part of face.
Action: Go to restroom, practice in mirror.

Symptom: Floor blurred.
Fault: You are looking through bottom of empty glass.
Action: Find buddy again.

Symptom: Room seems unusually dark.
Fault: Bar has closed.
Action: Confirm home address with bartender.

Symptom: Floor moving.
Fault: You are being carried out.
Action: Find out if you are being taken to another bar.

Symptom: Taxi suddenly takes on colorful aspect and textures.
Fault: Beer consumption has exceeded personal limitations.
Action: Cover mouth.

Symptom: Everyone looks up to you and smiles.
Fault: You are dancing on the table.

Action: Fall on somebody cushy looking.

Symptom: Beer is crystal clear.
Fault: It's water. Somebody is trying to sober you up.
Action: Punch him.

Symptom: Hands hurt, nose hurts, and mind's unusually clear.
Fault: You have been in a fight.
Action: Apologize to everyone you; see, just in case it was them.

Symptom: Don't recognize anyone, don't recognize room.
Fault: You've wandered into the wrong party.
Action: See if they have free beer.

Symptom: Your singing sounds distorted.
Fault: The beer is too weak.
Action: Have more beer until your voice improves.

Symptom: Don't remember the words to the song.
Fault: Beer just right.
Action: Play air guitar

Venison Swiss Steak –

"From my venison cookbook"

- 2 pounds venison round steak cut 1 inch thick
- 3 large yellow onions
- 1 ½ cup tomatoes
- ½ cup beer
- 1 cup flour
- 2 tablespoons Worcestershire sauce
- 1 tablespoon garlic salt
- 2 tablespoons black pepper

Roll the venison steak in flour and beat it with a hammer or tenderizer, you really have to pound it in. Season with garlic salt, Worcestershire sauce, and black pepper. Brown both sides slowly in a large skillet, add the tomatoes, beer, and onions (sliced)

Cover and simmer for about 30 minutes, or until done and gravy has thickened.

Right- Away- Ranch Beans –

- 6 cups water
- 1 pound dried pinto beans
- 1 can beer (dark)
- 1 cup chopped onion
- 6 bacon slices, cut into ½ inch pieces
- 4 garlic cloves, chopped
- 2 jalapeno peppers, chopped
- 1 cup chopped tomatoes
- ½ cup chopped fresh cilantro

Combine the water and next 6 ingredients in a large pot. Bring to boil and then simmer for about 3 hours.

Season to taste and top off with the tomatoes and cilantro before serving.

Venison Steak and Gravy –

- 3 pounds of venison cube steak
- 1 large yellow onion
- ½ cup beer (dark)
- 3 packages of brown gravy mix

In a large skillet, brown the cube steak. After browning, arrange the steaks in a baking pan. Chop the onion and add it to the steak. Make the gravy according to the package directions. Pour the gravy over the onion and add beer.

Cover with foil and bake at 400 degrees for about an hour. Serve with hash browns.

Deer in Beer –

" Yes another one from my cookbook! "So when are you going to buy it! You know you want to. Now immediately go to the back cover and order it! Or do you have to wait and see if momma gives you permission first. Man, and to think I talked about Becky's beaver, just for your enjoyment.

- 2 pounds deer roast
- ¼ teaspoon salt
- ¼ teaspoon black pepper *" Less, if you had to ask permission to buy my venison cookbook, you couldn't handle any more pepper.*
- 2 cans beer *"see above"*
- ½ cup brown sugar

- 2 tablespoons molasses
- 1 tablespoon garlic powder

Place meat in a large bowl and pour beer over it. Cover and marinate in refrigerator overnight.

Then, remove venison and pat dry, pour beer, sugar, garlic powder, and molasses in saucepan and cook over medium heat, stirring it until sugar dissolves.

Sprinkle the meat with salt and pepper and place in a large pan, then pour the beer mixture over it.

Cover with lid and bring to a boil, then reduce heat and simmer for two hours.

Coons In The Beer –

- 5 pounds coon meat, boneless
- 2 tablespoons butter
- 3 tablespoons flour
- ½ pound cheddar cheese, shredded
- 2 packages chopped broccoli
- ½ cup milk
- ½ cup beer
- 10 ounces sour cream
- 2 cans cream of mushroom soup

In a large pan cook coon and cut into pieces. Cook and drain broccoli.
Make sauce using the next remaining ingredients.

In a large baking pan layer half of meat, half of broccoli, half of sauce. Repeat with remaining half of ingredients.

Beer Corn Bread –

- 1 ½ cup beer (dark)
- 2 cups flour
- 1 cup cornmeal
- 3 ¾ teaspoon baking powder
- 2 tablespoons sugar

Preheat oven to 350 degrees. Mix ingredients together in a large bowl.

Pour batter into a greased loaf pan and bake for about 40 minutes.

Bubba's Beer Batter Bread –

- 3 cups flour
- 1 tablespoon baking powder
- 3 tablespoons sugar
- 1 teaspoon salt
- 1 can beer (room temperature)
- ¼ cup unsalted butter, melted

Preheat oven to 375 degrees. In a large mixing bowl, combine all the dry ingredients. Add beer.

Pour batter into a loaf pan and brush with melted butter. Bake in the oven for about 40 minutes.

Are you nuts! Man if you read these off to her, You're dead meat! Go ahead, I warned you.... Six-pack courage!

1. Beer doesn't care if you have no culture.
2. Beer doesn't cry.
3. Beer doesn't mine football season.

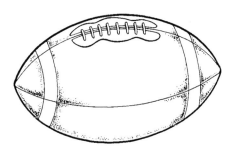

4. Beer doesn't drag you to church.
5. A beer is more likely to know how to spell "carburetor" than a woman.

6. Beer doesn't think baseball is stupid simply because the guys spit.

7. A beer doesn't care if you keep a bunch of other beer around in the garage.
8. Beer never complains when you take it somewhere.
9. Beer doesn't use up your toilet paper.
10. Beer doesn't make you put the lid down when you're done.
11. Beer will not insists that those odious Michelin commercials with babies are 'cute".
12. If a beer leaks all over the room, it smells kinda good for a while.
13. A beer will not call you a sexist pig.

14. A beer won't claim that the Three Stooges are disgusting.
15. A beer won't whine that the seatbelts hurt.
16. A beer never watches Opra.
17. A beer never fishes for compliments.
18. A beer won't smoke in your car.
19. A beer will never stop you from reading Playboy.
20. A beer likes to drive fast.

21. A beer loves the sound of straight pipes on a Harley.
22. A beer thinks coon-dogs are a good thing.
23. A beer never has to shave its legs.
24. A beer never sets you up by asking if its butt looks fat in a dress.

25. A beer will never make you see its parents.

I'm not done yet. Turn the page for information about others of my books.

See next page for an illustration of my Venison Cookbook.

VENISON
COOKBOOK

FOUR WHEELIN'

SLUG SLINGIN'

BEER DRINKIN'

ARROW SHOOTIN'

HELL RAISIN'

A REAL HE-MAN COOKBOOK WITH RECIPES
THAT USE DEAD THINGS, AND HOT STUFF,
AND PARTS OF PICKUP TRUCKS.

WITH THIS COOKBOOK, YOU CAN BE
A REAL HE-MAN!

BY RICK BLACK

See next page for an illustration of my FUNKY DUCK
DUCK COOKBOOK.

The

FUNKY DUCK

Duck COOKBOOK

DUCK HUNTIN'

DOGGIN'

CHAW CHEWIN'

BEER DRINKIN'

HELL RAISIN'

A REAL HE-MAN COOKBOOK WITH RECIPES
THAT USE DEAD THINGS, AND HOT STUFF,
AND PARTS OF PICKUP TRUCKS.

WITH THIS COOKBOOK, YOU CAN BE
A REAL HE-MAN!

BY RICK BLACK

See next page for an illustration of my BAG "EM AND TAG 'EM how-to book on deer hunting.

BAG 'EM

and

TAG 'EM

-all about deer huntin'

by Rick Black

To Order Copies

Please send me _____ copies:
at $9.95 each of *Cooking with Beer*
plus $2.00 S/H. (Make checks payable
to **BLACK IRON COOKING.**)

Name _____

Street _____

City _____ State _____ Zip _____

BLACK IRON COOKING
1854 - 345th Avenue
Wever IA   52658
1-800-571-2665

To Order Copies

Please send me _____ copies:
at $9.95 each of *Cooking with Beer*
plus $2.00 S/H. (Make checks payable
to **BLACK IRON COOKING.**)

Name _____

Street _____

City _____ State _____ Zip _____

BLACK IRON COOKING
1854 - 345th Avenue
Wever IA   52658
1-800-571-2665